The True Life of

With Her Birth, Education, and Adventures
with Some Account of Her Elder Sister Blanch of
Britain. Containing Sundry Very Curious Particulars

Anonymous

Alpha Editions

This edition published in 2024

ISBN : 9789362095862

Design and Setting By
Alpha Editions
www.alphaedis.com
Email - info@alphaedis.com

As per information held with us this book is in Public Domain.
This book is a reproduction of an important historical work. Alpha Editions uses the best technology to reproduce historical work in the same manner it was first published to preserve its original nature. Any marks or number seen are left intentionally to preserve its true form.

Contents

THE TRUE LIFE OF BETTY IRELAND. ....- 1 -

THE TRUE LIFE OF BETTY IRELAND.

It is agreed on all Hands, that *Betty Ireland* was a younger Daughter by a *second Venter*; let, at first, to run wild in the Woods, cloathed with Skins and fed with Acorns; till a *famous Hunter* took her in his Toils, and, liking her *Countenance*, gave her to a Son of his, a *Lad*, to bring up. The *Girl*[6] was born to a good Estate, but ill tenanted, and run to waste. Her *Farms* neither *meared* or bounded, her Rents never paid, as she had no *certain* Tenants, and had little more to claim than a Pepper-corn Acknowledgment. She had no Relation to manage her *Demesnes*, and could hardly be said to be possessed of any thing.

In this Condition the young *Sportsman* found her, was fond of her at first, and resolved to marry her; and *happy* had it been both for *him* and *her*, if he had kept his Resolution, and performed the *Contract*. But he hankered after his elder Brother's *Estate*, and, on his Death, suddenly got the Tenants to *attorn* to *him*, and basely dispossessed his *Nephew*. But instead of an *Estate*, he got nothing but a *Law-suit*, lived in *Broils*, and dyed a *Beggar*. Whereas had he quitted all Pretensions at home, married *Betty* and minded her Concerns, he had soon been in a Condition not to envy his Brother; and, perhaps, had left a *second Family*[7] little inferior in *Greatness* to the first.

This was the only Chance ever *Betty* had to make a *separate* Fortune, set up for herself, and be *independent* of her *Sister*. She was ever after *beholden* to *her* for maintaining her *Rights*, settling her *Affairs*, and bringing her *Tenants* to Reason.

Neither *Betty* or her Sister were yet of Age, but the Younger far from it, and continued under such *Guardians*, as the *Elder* recommended, and had chosen for herself. It was natural to think they should chiefly be employed in ordering the Affairs of *Blanch*, and be less attentive to benefit the other. Accordingly, from time to time, they sent *Proxies*, to let Leases, keep her *Courts*, and *force* Possession, where the Tenants held over. Little, however, was done for *Betty*, though they put her

Sister to great Charges; nor did she thrive in the World to any Purpose, 'till she came under the Care of a good *orderly Gentlewoman*, who was also *Guardian* to *Blanch*, a notable[8] *Manager*, and very affectionate to her *Wards*, understood their Business to a hair, and was never to be imposed on or *over-reached*. Every thing she put her hand to prospered, and every thing against her miscarried.

When she first looked into *Betty*'s Affairs, she found them in a manner desperate; her small Revenues had been embezzled by *Agents*, Farms set to *insolvent* Tenants, *double* Leases made out, huge *Fines* taken in Hand and sunk in their own Pockets. She was preyed upon by Vagabonds and *Outlaws*; and, to compleat her Misfortunes, a *Foreign Count* fell in love with her, an odious Monster and *braggadocio* Huffer. He swore bitterly no one else should have her, and to support his Claim, brought in his Pocket, a *pretended Licence* from the *Spiritual Court*, and a Pack of *outlandish Goths* along with him, to take Possession of her Freehold, and break down her Gates. But her *Sister* generously came in to her Assistance, repelled Force by Force, and rescued her from a Tyrant Ravisher, built Houses for herself, and Fences for the[9] Tenants, and left some of her own People with her to instruct them in Trades and Husbandry.

She was then, it might be thought, in a Way of making herself respected, both by her own and her *Sister*'s Tenants, and not stand in need of any more Supplies from them; and if the *good Woman*, her guardian, had lived to bring Matters to any Kind of Establishment, Things had been better. But she unfortunately died, more, however, to her *Sister*'s Disadvantage than *hers*; for the *Guardian* had chalked out a Track of Proceeding for *Betty*, which she could hardly miss to follow. The *Elder*, however, was inconsolable for the Loss of her *Guardian*, and resolved, for the future, to manage her Concerns by the Assistance of a *Steward*, a Sort of a Cousin to her *Guardian* deceased, but no way allied to her, in Worth or Understanding. He minded nothing but Hunting and *Puppet-shews*, Feasts and Revels; and though the uncomeliest of an *ill-*

favoured Race, spent his Lady's Money in adorning his own Person, instead[10] of *fencing* her Grounds. He was laughed at by one half of the Neighbours, and despised and gulled by the other. In a Word, he was every Way unfit for the Charge.

His Son succeeded to the Place; he was a grave-looking, orderly young Man, main religious, and skilled in the *Customs of the Manor*. Both the Sisters had great Hopes their Affairs would thrive under his Management. *Betty*'s, indeed, went on well for a while; but, in the End, both of them had Cause to complain, and curse the Day they had bethought them of employing a *Steward* in their Concerns. He was not so great a Fool as his Father; yet nothing he put his Hand to succeeded. He was *bubbled* by every *Neighbour* he dealt with, and choused by every *Tenant* he trusted. His Word could never be relied on, as he had always some quibble to evade it. His Wife made him hated by the Tenants; and for a finishing Stroke to his undoing, and compleat the Ruin of his *Wards*, he pretended the *Steward* had a Right to hold Courts without *Juries*, and by his own[11] Authority levy Money for *Repairs*. The Tenants would not endure this Invasion on their Rights, but stoutly opposed it; and, after a hard Struggle, got the better, turned him out of the *Stewardship*, and some of them finding him one Day at a *why-not*, tied him to a Rope, and hanged him in a Frolick.

The Office of a *Steward* was now abolished for a Time, and the elder *Sister* resolved to take her Affairs entirely into her *own Hands*, and have neither *Steward* or *Guardian* for the future. The Condition, indeed, of *both* was deplorable. There had been nothing during the *late Quarrel*, but Riot and Plunder, Rents unpaid, and Soldiers quartered at Discretion; so that, in order to retrieve their Affairs, it seemed necessary to put things on a *new Footing*, and trust none but themselves to manage them. But whatever they intended mattered but little.

Among the Soldiers quartered on them was a bustling Knave, who from a Corporal had come to be a Captain. He was bold as a Lion,[12] and *crafty* as a Fox. He had cajoled his Soldiers to stand by him; and pretending *Compassion* for the Sisters, offered, or rather forced himself, to be their *Guardian*. They only complied because they could not help it; and he took more *rule* over them, than ever *Steward* or *Guardian* had done before him.

He seemed, indeed, to mend Matters in the Beginning, but, in reality, did *unrepairable* Damage to *Blanch*, though considerable Services to *Betty*. The Neighbours all around thought they were thriving apace, and began to envy their Greatness. The Reason of which was, that he always took care to have the *Girls* well dressed, especially when they went a *visiting*, and sent Word before-hand (for he was d——d proud) that all the World should *Cap* to them as they passed along. He stinted them in every thing else, but *spent* all he could *rap* and *run* to make them *fine*. *Betty* was *bashful*, and kept pretty much at home; but when *Blanch* went *abroad*, she made a *flaming* Appearance, *held* up her Head among the *Highest*, and *insulted*[13] the *Proudest* with her *Braveries*.

But all the while Things were but *uncomfortable* at home, though she made such a *tearing Figure* when abroad. Nothing to be had for Farms, by reason the Soldiers put *in* and *out* as they pleased. No *Leets* or *Manor Courts* were minded. No *taxing* for *Repairs* and *Bounds*, but the Soldiers *taxed* for *Contingencies* as much Money as they could hear any one had. So that the *Tenants* found themselves in a worse *Pickle* than ever they had been under the Management of a *Steward*. They longed for Courts and *Inquests*, and to have every thing set on the old Bottom again.

They heard of a *poor Boy*, a Son of the late *Steward*'s, who had run away from the *Lands* the Time his Father was hanged, and was now grown up to Years of Discretion. As he had *bit* a good while on the Bridle, they thought he might be tamed, more careful than his *Father*, and do them more Justice and Kindness. They brought him home in a *Hurry*; and, as it's natural[14] to run from one Extreme to another, were sure they were all *made* when they got him into the *Stewardship*.

It must be owned, he was a pleasant, good-humoured Fellow as ever broke Bread, civilly behaved, and by no means wanted Capacity for the Business. But he was *idle* to a Degree, followed W———ng and Horse-racing; and provided he could borrow Money enough from the *Tenants*, or get *Presents* from the *Neighbours*, to treat his Wenches and buy them *Top-knots*, never heeded how *Accounts* were settled, how he held the *Courts*, or how he paid the Servants. Farm-houses went to decay, and Strangers forestalled the Markets. Few People, however, could find in their Heart to hate him. They had a Love for him, though he was daily undoing them: For it was always *their Humour* to like a *boon Companion*; and instead of crossing his Prodigality, they followed his Example, wh——ed it away from the highest to the lowest, revelled and caroused for *dear Blood*, and were never better pleased than when the last Penny[15] was a going. It became a *Fashion* to be Bankrupt; to be Rich, was to lose all Credit; and to be Just, was the Mark of a Scoundrel.

But though the *elder Sister* was well-nigh undone by him, he did a good Turn by *Betty*, and sent one of his *Cousins* to take care of her Concerns, who had a good Farm of his own under her, and was well-beloved over the whole Estate. He kept *Leet* and *Court-Baron*, presented Vagabonds at the Sessions, and gave Rewards for apprehending *Out-laws*. He set the Tenants to Work, *lived constantly among them*, and looked himself into every thing. *Betty* began to thrive, and was less expensive to her *Sister*, who had wasted huge Sums to keep her Head above Water. She stuck to Business, and prospered mainly, 'till the *Steward*'s Brother got himself into the Place, who played H———ll with every thing, and brought the two Sisters to the Brink of Ruin.

He was rash, senseless, obstinate, and ill-minded;[16] none of the Neighbours would *deal* with him, or the *Tenants* trust him, as there was no believing one Word he said, or promise that he made; for he had taken an Oath when he was young never to speak Truth. He began his Vagaries by putting the *Curate* in the *Stocks*, for refusing to teach a new *Catechism* of his *own*

Invention. He entered into a Plot to secure the *Elder Sister* in the House of Correction, and make her do Penance in the Church, under Pretence of Carnal Conversation. He agreed to sell *Betty* to a Cousin of his, a great Lord in the Neighbourhood, who longed to have her for a Waiting-woman to his Wife. So the *Tenants* made short Work with him, rose one and all, and sent him a-packing to his Cousin, where he was fain to be a Serving-man, since he could not send *Betty* to be a Serving-maid.

Both the *Sisters* took an Oath never more to have a *Steward* again, and to abolish the very Name from among them, with a reserve to his Daughters, who had married abroad, and were[17] good sort of Women, in their Way.

Here it was that *both the Sisters* had their Affairs put on a sure and lasting Footing. The Rights of the *Tenants* were narrowly examined, and all pretended Powers of the Steward abolished by a Rule on the *Court Manor* Books. There was, indeed, some Difficulty in bringing it about, and a power of Money laid out on the Occasion. But it was well bestowed had it been twice as much.

There was a *Stripling* among the neighbouring *Fens*, who had married a Daughter of the *Steward*'s, and had got the best Estate there by the Diligence of his *Ancestors*, who were the principal *Engineers* in *draining* and *banking* the Country. They had often borrowed Money from *Blanch* to carry on the Work, to *stem* the Water when the *Fen-men* were in despair, and prevailed on her to send a strong *Posse* of her Tenants to keep off some malicious Neighbours, who would ever and anon be *boring* Holes in the *Dikes*, and endangered the Overflowing[18] of all the Land they had gained. If ever these *wretched People* shewed any thing that looked like *Gratitude*, it was to the Family of their *Engineers*; and this young Man improved it to his own Advantage, and that of *Blanch*, whom he acknowledged the Preserver of the *Fen-men*, who deserved Preservation on no other Account than to make them *Pack-horses* and *Carriers*. They were, indeed, a middle Species between Men and Brutes, and chiefly compounded of the latter. But this young *Adventurer* had got the Ascendant over them, and, as we ordinarily say of vicious Horses, had made the D——l come out of them. He *ringed* them by the Nose, and *bled* them with the *Spur*, and so throughly *broke* them (for he was a special Horseman) that they never kicked or plunged when he was *in the Saddle*; but, as the Nature of Beasts is, became the fonder of him the rougher he handled them.

When he understood that *Blanch* and her *Sister* were so hampered and *Tyrannically* treated by the *Steward*, he came to their Assistance, supplied[19] them with Money, which he raised from the *Fen-men*, and fairly set them free from his Oppression and Rapine, reversed his *Grants*, cancelled his sham Leases, restored Possessions, *Leets* and *Manor-Courts*, made up *Fences* for the Tenants, and so strongly secured their *Copyholds*, that there is no likelihood they will ever be *ousted* or much *disturbed* again. And, to crown all the Services he had done the two Sisters, he *recommended* them, before he parted, to the Care of a *neighbouring Lord*, a Cousin of his own, and a *right honest Man*, who proved a Father to *them* and their People, defended their *Rights*, and secured their *Properties*.

And yet *Blanch* could never rightly like the *Fen-man*, as she called him, though he had done so much for her. She could not comport herself with his Manners and his Humour, hated the Servants he brought with him, complained they were too costly to her, though she kept them sparingly, and even quarrelled (so exceptious are Women) to the Cut of their[20] Cloaths, and the Colour of their *Liveries*.

But *Betty Ireland* had more Gratitude than her *Sister*, adored him while he stayed with her, and to this Day *remembers* him as her *great Deliverer*, the Protector of her Life, and the Founder of her Fortune.

She, indeed, had double Obligations, as her Condition was more helpless than her *Sister*'s, and she had more severely felt the *Tyranny* of the *Steward*, who, because she could not so readily complain of him, had first *stripped* her of all she had, and then sold her to Bondage. But both *Sisters* ought surely to reflect, that all the Happiness, and all the Security they have since enjoyed, has been owing to the *Friendships* he procured them, when he put them under the Protection of *his Cousins*; and that he has effectually banished the *Stewards* thereby, who would doubtless otherwise be meddling with their Affairs, and use them worse than ever they did before, as coming *in without Leave*, they would[21] act without Controul.

But maugre all these Considerations, *Blanch* was glad when he left her, and ready to leap out of her Skin for joy. She thought of nothing but Diversions, spent her *Time* and *Money* in *visiting* and *dressing*, ransacked the Globe to set off her Person, and, it must be owned, she never looked handsomer in her Life. Wherever she went, she was adored as an Angel, surrounded by admiring Throngs, and Thousands hanging on her *Look*.

But all this was empty Pageantry and too expensive Glory. She ran herself in Debt to uphold this Appearance, mortgaged her *Estate*, and bartered her *Stock*, for the vain Applause of flattering Knaves, and scoundrel *Tradesmen*. It was Time to pull in, and keep a Hank in the Hand. She saw her Folly, and doffed her *Gear*. It was better *go plain* than run in Debt for Finery; and enough she had to do to pay the Debts she had contracted in her *Fit of* Vanity.

Betty all the while was minding Business[22] at home, and her Affairs prospered amain. Her *Tenants* became industrious, and her *Estate* improved; yet she never thought herself sufficiently *secure* till she got under the new *Protection* her *Deliverer* had provided. Her Situation is particular. She has a strange Mixture of People on her Estate, who are always at Daggers drawing with one another, and a mighty Hindrance to her Business. They are *Whites*, *Blacks*, and *Black and White*. The *Whites* only are allowed to be *Land-holders*; but the *last*, by hiding half the Face when they converse with her, pass for *Whites*, and make good their *Titles*. The first are dreadfully maligned by the *Blacks*, who are unhappily the more numerous, *lay old Claims* to her *Lands*, and are ever watching for an Opportunity to make a *Riot*, and take forcible Possession. 'Till now they were too much favoured by her *Sister*, which checked the Industry of her Farmers.

But when they found they had nothing to[23] fear, either at home or abroad, they began in earnest to improve *their Concerns*, as they were sure they were working for themselves, and in no Danger of being dispossessed, by Virtue of *chimerical* Claims, and *Antediluvian Proprietors*.

The *Blacks*, indeed, immediately made a *Riot* on this new Settlement, but could not get Possession; and, lately, a *young Jackanapes* pretended a *Right* to be *Steward* to *both Sisters*, by Virtue of a *Patent* he had got from the last *Steward*, as if he had a Right to dispose of a *Place* he had been turned out of himself. He came on the Lands, however, with a *bloody-minded* Crew of *skirtless* Vagabonds, drove off the Cattle, robbed the *Hen-roosts*, and *swaggered* at so *unmerciful* a Rate, that *Blanch* was frightened out of her Senses, and was fain to *send* for a Dram of *Gin* to restore her Spirits. But if she was frightened, her *Guardian* was not, and had a *Month's Mind* to find out the *Varlet* in Person, and tread him under his Feet. But as he could not leave the *Hall-house* where the[24] *Court was sitting*, he sent a *Lad* of his own to take Account of him, who did the *Business tightly*. He was a *well-mettled Blade*, and *Steel* to the *Back*. He came up with him at the Corner of a Farmer's Yard, where he gave him and his *Desperados* a wofull Drubbing, kicked him i'the A——e, *soused* him in the *Horse-pond*, which he swam over to save his Bacon, and looked so miserably scared in his Passage, that it's sure he'll never *try the Ford* again.

For a good while before this Alarm happened (which proved nothing but a *Bugbear*) both the *Sisters* had a fair Opportunity of minding their Concerns, and getting above the World. *Blanch* might have paid her Debts, and had Money to the fore; but it was ever her Misfortune to be *ill-served* by almost all she employed. Never, sure, had Lady so *unhandy* a Pack about her, and, indeed, it was impossible it could well be otherwise; for she did not chuse her *Servants* because they were *fit* for this, or that *Office*, but because they asked, and would have it, or be horribly out of Humour else, would make a[25] Noise and *Uproar* at every *Court-Leet*, terrify the *Tenants* at every *Ale-house*, with strange Stories of Designs on their *Copy-holds*, and wicked *Plots* just ready to begin; 'till they turned their Heads, and set them madding. So that the poor Lady was fain to *take them in*, to keep Peace at Home, and to pay them Wages for not doing her Business. The Consequence of which was, she had *Clerks* could neither write or read; Book, and Cash-keepers, that could not *count* or cast up, or ever heard of a *Ballance* in their Lives. And so ridiculous was her Compliance in this Point, that she had once a Lady to curry her Horse, and a *Fishmonger* for a *Grass Bailiff*.

'Tis true, she would often change her Servants, but not a *Barrel the better Herring*. If she got one, by chance, knew any thing of his Business, the *rest* never left boddering her 'till they had him out. It should never be said they demeaned themselves so much as to serve with one, who would spoil every thing by his *Rashness*, and disgrace the Service by his *Ignorance*.[26] Now, by *Rashness* they meant *resenting Insults* and *Injuries* done their Lady; and by *Ignorance*, not knowing how to *buy* and *sell*, and live by the *Loss*. So that, all Things considered, it were a Marvel her Affairs should be in better Plight than they are, or her Debts be paid with more Ease and Expedition.

Betty, in the mean time, is come to an opulent Fortune, has her Rents well paid, and her Farms daily improving, and would improve ten times more, if her *Sister* could see her own Advantage so far, as to give her that Encouragement she is daily giving to *Strangers*, who give her nothing in Return but their Envy and Ill-will. But as it is, *Betty*'s in a good Way, and makes the most of a bad Market. And since she must not work for her *Sister*, she works for herself.

It had been a Custom of hers to buy every thing she wanted from her *Sister's Tenants* and *Tradesmen*, though they used her abominably, and put off upon her the worst Goods they had.[27] If the Farmer had damaged Hops, he sold them to *Betty Ireland*; if his Malt was blinked, away it went to her; and the *Pothecary* thought his decayed Drugs good enough for *Betty*, and instead of burning them, laid them by for her, as tho' she were not a Christian, or had the same Inside as her Sister.

Betty could not help this contemptuous Treatment, as she had nothing she wanted at Home, by reason of her Laziness, though all Materials in abundance were at hand. 'Tis incredible to relate, but, at the Time I am speaking of, certain Fact, on her whole Estate there was not one to be found could make a Buckle for her Shoe, or a Pin to her Sleeve; a Pot, a Spit, or any Utensil to cook her Victuals, might as well be found among the *Tartars* as with her. She took every thing from her *Sister* at what Price she pleased, unsight unseen, and bought the *Pig in the Poke*. Necessity roused her from Stupidity and Sloth, she encouraged her Tenants to apply to Trades, assured them of a ready Market, and rewarded[28] those that did their Work the best; and, at present, has every thing within herself. And tho' it must be owned a very unreasonable, and *not to be endured* Instance of her Impudence, she proposes to dress in her own Manufactures, and does not mean to trouble her *Sister* any longer for *cast Cloaths* and *unmerchantable* commodities. But in every other Respect, she desires to keep up a good Correspondence with her, and is daily doing every thing in her Power, to gain her Favour, and procure her Regards. Whatever she can spare from her ordinary Expences, she, in some Shape or other, makes a Present of to her *Sister*, in Acknowledgement for Services done, and Kindnesses receiv'd in her *Minority*. Has *Blanch* a Favourite whom she cannot readily provide for, a poor Relation on hand, or Retainer to the Family, a broken Projector, or cast Serving-man; she has no more to do but acquaint *Betty* with it, who quickly puts him on a *creditable Pension*, and never refuses, though she run herself in Debt by it. Is *Blanch* engaged in a Brangle with her *Tenants*, (who, by the way, are cursedly litigious) and hard put to it for Hands to do her[29] Business, *Betty* makes an Offer of sending her People to help her, and maintaining them abroad at her own Charges. Does a Tenant of *Blanch* come to favour her with a Visit, she receives him with Hospitality and Respect, and would sacrifice her Fortune to make his Entertainment agreeable.

If all this Complaisance should fail of its Effect, and not so succeed as to keep *Blanch* in good Humour, 'tis easy to say where the Fault must lie, and from what Causes her Discontents arise.

In the first Place, it has ever been the Fate of her *Domesticks* to be invincibly hated by her *Tenants* without Difference or Distinction, (for, to say Truth, they have no Head for *Distingo*'s:) There is but one Thing in the World they hate more, and that is *Betty Ireland*. Now, the *Servants* bear hard on *Betty*, to curry Favour with her Sister's *Tenants*, who would go half Way to the D———l to have *Betty* d———d, are for ever cursing her, and laying all their Misfortunes at her Door. If the *Clothier* loses his Business, or has his[30] Goods on Hand, 'tis *all 'long of Betty*: Wheat bears no Price, for *Betty* has glutted the Market. Whereas, in Fact, they never keep the same Markets. But they forget, they are all so idle and debauched, such gobling and drinking Rascals, and so expensive in *blew Beer*, that they are forced to put a double Price on every thing goes to Market; so that no Body will deal with them. Indeed, if it incenses them, that *Betty* won't buy, burn her *own Goods* and take off *theirs*, they must e'en turn the Buckle behind. *Blanch* will be wiser, for her own sake, than lay Stresses on her *Sister*, from whom she gets more than *by all the World beside*, only to humour a Set of grumbling Churls, who don't know what they would be at; and so extremely senseless, that it's Matter of Wonder, their Oxen don't ride them to the Market, and sell them. 'Tis true, a *Linen-weaver*, one of *Blanch*'s Tenants, prevailed on her lately to withdraw some Encouragement she had given *Betty*, and transfer it to a *Stranger*. But that was owing to bad Advice given her, by a *Clerk* she has since turned off, and sent a stroling among *Brandy-shops*[31] and *Ale-houses*, to *backbite* his *Lady* for want of other Employment.

Another Cause of *Blanch*'s Dislike to her *Sister* was, a Fright she took, when she was just *delivered*, at some ill-looking People, who came from *Betty*'s Lands, and appeared under her Window. There's no doubt but *Blanch* has as much Courage as any genteel Lady ought to have, and must have been in a Fit of low Spirits when she, and all her Tenants from her, took so senseless an alarm, as to run distracted thro' Fear of half a Dozen Fellows cutting all their Throats in one Night, who were ready to run through Fire and Water for Fear of being hang'd themselves; yet certain it is, from this ridiculous Incident, and from nothing else, can be derived, that universal Hatred shewn her by *Blanch's Tenants*, though they have never seen, spoken with, or had any Dealings whatever, either with *Betty* or her *Tenants*. People must be *generous*, as well as *brave*, to forgive those that frighten them.

There's another Cause of Dislike among[32] such as have Dealings with *Betty*'s Tenants who come on Business, or to visit her *Sister*, that they run in debt with them, and don't pay. So do all their Neighbours, for that matter; but they complain of none but *Betty*, though it is very well known they make ample Reprisals on her; and *one Bite* of theirs, is worth a hundred of *Betty*'s, who are none but such as are despised at home, and can get neither Credit or Company there; for *Betty* is not yet arrived to that Degree of Politeness, as to court and caress *Highway-men* and *Sharpers*, only because *they keep good Company*, and are Gentlemen of *nice Honour*, but sincerely wishes her *Sister* to hang them all.

The last I shall mention (and, to be sure, a wise Cause of Dislike it is) *Betty* goes once, at least, every Year to pay her Sister a Visit, carries all her Money, puts on her best Cloaths, lives high as long as she has a Penny left. This vexes her *Sister*, and many a *Slut* and *Flirt* she calls *Betty*, at the very time she is throwing away her[33] Money with both Hands for the Tradesmen and Shoeboys to scramble up. They are both Fools; *One* for shewing this Contempt, and the other for putting herself in the Way of it.

It is wished, but probably in vain, that the two *Sisters* would come to a better Understanding. They that have considered the true Interest of both, see plainly that the *elder*, and consequently the *younger*, must be shortly undone, if these Bickerings and ill Offices continue. So *unnatural* a Quarrel between near Relations must make them despised by all the *Neighbours* around, who are hourly taking the Advantage of it, and *profiting* themselves by the Hindrance the *Sisters* give to each other. But their Manners and Disposition are so different, that it's next to impossible they should ever love one another; tho', for mutual Interest, and to make that Figure in the Eye of the World which two *Ladies* of their Distinction and Fortune ought to assume, their Friends may agree to promote *jointly* their Interests, and never heed how peevish and untoward *either* of them may be, or pay any Regard to the[34] *fanciful Aversions*, and ungrounded Jealousies, which are always inseparable from a female Breast.

Tho' in this History I have rather copied the *chaste Brevity* of *Cornelius Nepos*, than the diffused and *chatty* Eloquence of *Plutarch*; I shall conclude, in Imitation of the latter, with a Description of the two *Ladies*, their Persons, Manners, and Inclinations; and, in drawing the *Parallel*, with Freedom represent, their Vices as well as *Vertues*, their Faults as well as their Perfections.

Blanch is by much the taller, neat, timbersome, and well made, a lively Look and a sprightly Air. *Betty's* Face is full out as *handsome* as her *Sister*'s, tho' not so regular, has more *variety* and striking Beauties, and, with equal *Dressing*, would appear more lovely than the other; but she's a *Slattern* in her *Dress*.

As to their *Tempers*, *Pride* is the prevailing Passion of the *first*, and *Vanity* of the *second*; from which naturally, and unavoidably arises,[35] every observable Character of their Mind and Manners. *Blanch's* Pride makes her selfish and reserved, contemptuous, if not rough, in her Behaviour. *Betty's* Vanity makes her *open* and communicative, fond of *shewing herself* on all Occasions, complaisant, and caressing, to a Degree of

Flattery. As *Blanch* does not know what it is to have Love or Affection for any one but herself, so she expects it from no one, but claims a great deal of Respect. *Betty* doesn't know what Respect for her means, but to gain her Love and Liking would part with all she had. *Blanch* is frugal in the main, not very hospitable, and seldom lavish but in private Pleasures. *Betty* is hospitable to Prodigality, lavish to Folly, and thinks nothing a Pleasure that others don't share in. Hence it comes, that the first loves her Money above all things, the *second* less than any thing she has any value for at all; that one is anxious to *get*, the *other* in haste to *spend*. *Blanch* has a good Understanding, but does not *know the World*, and is commonly *choused* by her Neighbours. *Betty* has no Opportunity of *knowing the World*, as her *Sister* won't let her go[36] much abroad or converse with the *Neighbours*; she has but little Experience, and, to be sure, is not very *wise*, but is the quickest in the World at finding out *a Fool*. The *elder* is *cautious*, and hides carefully every Fault she is conscious of; the *younger* is not conscious of any Fault of Folly whatever; so they all come out in her *communicative Fits*, which seize her as often as she gets a Stranger to talk to. *Blanch* is the more censorious, and *Betty* the greater Liar.

If either of the *Ladies* think the Picture not like, let them call to mind the Story of a famous Painter, who had drawn the Portrait of a young Man, who stood very well with himself, but didn't please him. "You have drawn me," said he, "exactly the *Reverse* of every thing I am." *If it be so*, replied the Painter, *that must be your Likeness*, and set the Picture on the Head.

FINIS.

Milton Keynes UK
Ingram Content Group UK Ltd.
UKHW040840141024
449705UK00006B/398